Riley Pie, the Lovable Pup

Elida Y. Garcia-DeHaan

Copyright © 2018 Elida Y. Garcia-DeHaan

All rights reserved.

ISBN: 1727025350
ISBN-13: 978-1727025354

DEDICATION

This book is dedicated to my Riley Pie. You helped me relearn to love and trust big dogs once again.

Riley Pie and his Mom

CONTENTS

Information for other books written by the author
pg. 21
About the Author   pg. 22

Riley Pie at 8 months old

Riley looking at his daddy while they were on the balcony.

This is Riley Pie with his dad who happens to be his handler. Before Riley Pie became a service dog, he was a family dog who loves going swimming. Before he became a service dog, he was a family dog.

His dad started to notice Riley Pie help him with every task around the house especially when he was in pain.

One day his dad taught him to pick up items that fell on the floor. The first task he taught him was to pick up a water bottle.

Sometimes Riley Pie lies in bed next to his daddy especially when dad is having a hard time trying to sleep. Other times Riley decides to lay in the bed on his own every morning.

Riley Pie loves listening to music. Every now and then he will howl along to the music.

He loves going for walks with his dad, and meeting new people while he is out for a walk.

One night while Riley Pie and his dad were out for a walk at night, Riley started to growl while looking towards one of the trees behind their house.

He could sense there was danger and tried directing his dad back in the house, but his dad decided to shine the flashlight in the direction were Riley Pie was growling.

As soon as the light hit the tree, his dad noticed three sets of eyes watching them. There were three raccoons over by the tree, and Riley Pie's dad walked Riley back into the house and called him a good boy for letting him that there were other animals out there.

Before Riley Pie started showing signs of service dog, Riley Pie started showing signs of a hunting dog.

Although he has never been hunting, he knew what scents to smell and track. Ultimately his mom and dad started buying him toys that represent certain type of animals Labrador retrievers usually hunt for.

One day out of the blue he picked a bird decoy toy the way a hunting dog is supposed to pick up a bird while hunting. He did not need any special training in that area hunting.

His favorite spot in the house is the recliner, or lying next to his dad's chair.

His favorite time of the day is meal time. He gets fed three times a day in order to stay healthy and strong.

Sometimes he likes to goof around and wear baseball caps while posing for pictures.

During football season he wears a doggy sports jersey for his parents' favorite team whenever the game is on.

Riley Pie is a very lovable pup. He loves kids and helping around the house. This drawing represents the bond Riley Pie has with one of his mom's cousin's sons.

ABOUT THE AUTHOR

Elida Y. Garcia-DeHaan is a loves her dogs to the moon and back, and hopes to share their stories with the world in order keep their memories alive long after they have crossed the rainbow bridge.

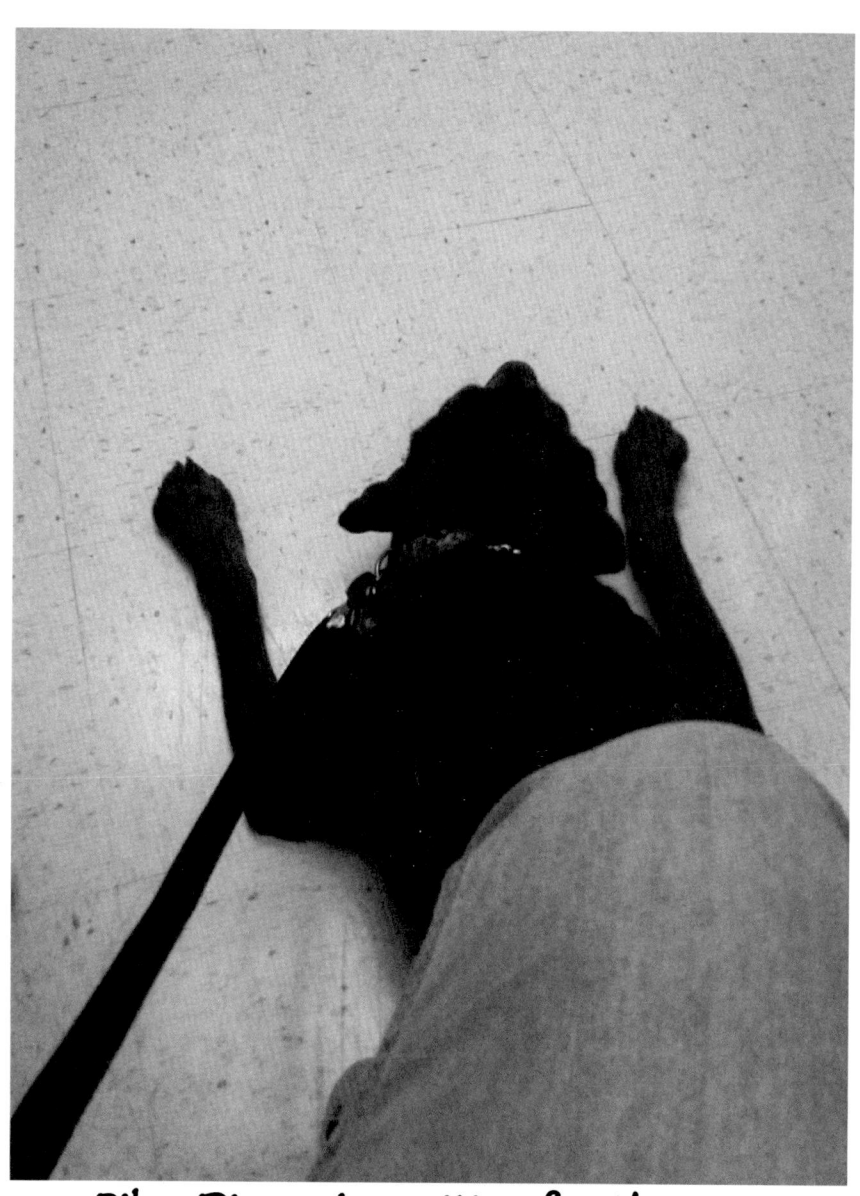

Riley Pie and I waiting for the vet.

My Riley Pie as a puppy

Made in the USA
Middletown, DE
27 March 2019